RICE & BREADS

SRI LANKAN STYLE

Recipes by Shyamali Perera

Series 1

Copyright

Copyright©2020 Shyamali Perera
All rights reserved

No part of this book may be used, reproduced, transmitted or sold in whole or part in any form (print or digital) without the written consent from the author.

All art work in this book, owned by Shyamali Perera. All photography credit to Shyamali Perera, Adobe Stock, BigStock, and Shutterstock royalty free stock photography.

Disclaimer

The material presented in this book is for informational purposes only. Please note that some ingredients mentioned in this book might not agree with first time users and food tasters.

Dedication

To everyone who lost their lives during the global pandemic COVID-19 of 2019-2020.

To everyone who offered their services daily, to help us live through these difficult times.

To John Perera, my paternal grandfather, who I never met because he couldn't survive the last global pandemic of 1920.

May all souls departed, rest in peace, and be guided to the "Divine Light".

TABLE OF CONTENTS

INTRODUCTION 8

RICE 11

KAHA BUTH-YELLOW RICE 12

CHICKEN BIRYANI & RICE 15

FRIED RICE 18

KIRI BUTH-MILK RICE 21

SIYAMBALA BUTH-TAMARIND RICE 23

BREADS 25

KOTTU-ROTI 26

POL-ROTI COCONUT FLAT BREAD 29

PITTU 31

APPA (HOPPERS) 32

INDI APPA (STRING HOPPERS) 34

THOSAI 36

EQUIPMENT LIST 38

ACKNOWLEDGMENTS 39

ABOUT THE AUTHOR 39

INTRODUCTION

Ayubowan. Sri Lanka is a pear-shaped island tucked away in the Indian Ocean, below India. To the seventh-century Arabian spice merchants, it was known as Serendip, and to the European conquerors and explorers, Ceylon or the Pearl of the Indian Ocean. Sri Lanka boasts of not only a variety of climates but also well-adapted cultural influences.

Sri Lanka's history dates before the time of the Buddha when the aboriginal tribes of the Yakkas and the Nagas ruled the land and were a part of the ancient Asian civilization. It is chronicled in the Mahawansa that the Buddha visited Sri Lanka on several occasions in the fifth century BC to preach to these tribes amidst their ongoing wars. Although Sri Lanka has fought many battles during the past 2500 years, the island has been blessed with tropical beauty, an abundance of food and rare aromatic spices. Folklore and folk tales depict, that these rare herbs and spices as being brought to the island by the demigod Hanuman for medicinal purposes during the great battle between Ravana, the Yakka king, and the Hindu deity Rama.

A variety of spices and herbs are used in Sri Lankan cooking. But the cooking styles have a marked difference according to the region of origin. The north and east of the country have cuisines with prominent south Indian flavors, and the hill country is flavored with hill-grown fruits and vegetables. The west and coastal areas boast of cuisines with an abundance of fresh fish and vegetables.

The use of these spices can be considered a personal style and preference; therefore, exact measurements and quantities are deemed unnecessary. Hence the Sri Lankan cook throws in a pinch of this and a pinch of that and wham-bam......the outcome is mouth-watering food, layered with a multitude of flavors. The famous Sri Lankan curry refers to a variety of flavorful dishes cooked mostly with coconut milk and is eaten usually with rice. The recipes in this book are written with an international audience in mind and can be changed to suit one's palate.

Hope you have a great culinary experience using these recipes.

RICE

KAHA BUTH-YELLOW RICE

Ingredients

- 1 pound basmati rice (3 1/2 cups of rice)
- 3 onions
- 6 cardamoms
- 6 cloves
- 6 peppercorns
- ¼ cup ghee
- 1 sprig curry Leaves
- ½ inch stem lemon grass
- 1 cup coconut milk
- 1 inch cinnamon stick
- ½ teaspoon turmeric powder
- salt to taste

Directions

1. Wash the rice. Slice the onions and grind the cardamoms, cloves and peppercorns together. Heat the ghee and when hot, fry the onion, curry leaves and lemon grass, until onions are browned, then add the rice and stir fry for further 3 minutes.
2. Add ground peppercorn mix, coconut milk, turmeric powder, salt and warm water as required and bring to boil. Cook over high heat for approximately 5 minutes, then reduce heat, cover pan and simmer until rice is cooked. Serve with any curry of your choice.

CHICKEN BIRYANI & RICE

Ingredients / Chicken

- 1 whole chicken
- 2/3 cups onion
- 2 fresh chilies
- 1/4 cup coconut
- 2/3 cup fresh cashew nuts
- 1/4 cup raisins
- 2 cloves and
- 2 cardamoms
- 4 eggs
- ¼ cup tomato paste
- ¼ cup yogurt
- ½ teaspoon turmeric powder
- 1 teaspoon paprika powder
- 1 teaspoon chili powder
- 3 teaspoons curry powder
- 1 inch cinnamon stick
- ¼ cup oil
- ¼ cup water
- 2 sprigs curry leaves
- 1 teaspoon salt

Ingredients / Rice

- ½ pound basmati rice (1 3/4 cups of raw rice)
- 3 onions
- 3 cardamoms
- ½ cup oil
- sprig curry leaves
- ½ teaspoon turmeric powder
- 2 ¼ cup chicken stock

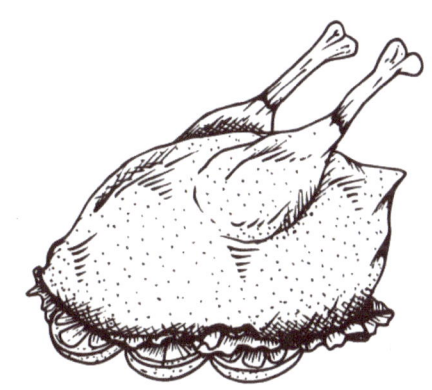

Directions

1. Wash, dry and joint the chicken. Chop the onion and chilies. Grate the coconut and chop half of the cashew nuts finely. Grind the cloves and cardamoms.
2. Boil the eggs, shell them and sprinkle with turmeric and ½ tsp salt. In a blender place the coconut, the chopped nuts, cloves, cardamoms, tomato paste, yoghurt, paprika, chili powder, curry paste, cinnamon stick and remaining salt.
3. Blend into a smooth paste then add to the chicken pieces and set aside to marinate for 10-15 minutes.
4. Heat the oil and fry onion, curry leaves and chili for 3 minutes. Add the chicken pieces and fry for a further 5-10 minutes. Add the water to the chicken marinade, pour into the pan and simmer.
5. Meanwhile, prick the eggs with a toothpick and fry in a little oil until light brown. Remove, drain and in the same oil fry the remaining nuts. When the chicken is cooked pile it into the center of a serving dish. Surround it with rice and eggs and garnish with cashew nuts and raisins.
6. Save the chicken stock to prepare the rice.

To Prepare Rice

1. Wash and drain rice. Chop onion and crush the cardamoms and cloves. Heat the oil, add the onion, curry leaves and lemon grass and when fragrant add the cardamoms, cloves, cinnamon stick and turmeric.
2. When its light brown in color, add the rice and cook for a few minutes until the rice begins to crackle. Pour in the stock and cook until the rice is soft and a bit sticky.

- Optional: Sliced tomato and cilantro can be used to garnish the rice.
- Grated coconut is available in Asian grocery stores.

FRIED RICE

Ingredients

- 1/2 pound rice (1 3/4 cups)
- 1/4 cup grated carrots
- 1/4 cup leek chopped finely
- 1/4 cup white cabbage chopped finely
- 2 shallots chopped finely
- 2 cloves of garlic chopped finely
- 2 slices ginger chopped finely
- 3/4 cup organic coconut oil or vegetable oil
- 1 tablespoon ground black pepper
- 4 eggs
- salt to taste

Directions

1. Wash and drain rice and cook in Rice Cooker or on the stovetop. Spoon rice well when cooked and serve on to a rectangle dish and spread it well so the rice cools and is not sticky.
2. Heat 1/4 cup oil of your choice in a large skillet and add the chopped onions, garlic, ginger, salt and stir fry till brown. Slowly add the carrots and stir fry for 5 mins till soft. Then add the finely chopped leek and cabbage and stir fry till the vegetables are transparent and glossy. Transfer to a dish and set aside to cool for a few minutes.
3. Heat 1/4 cup oil in the same skillet and add a spoon full of rice and vegetables at a time and mix well while cooking. Lower the heat to medium to low while mixing the rice and vegetables so the mixture does not get burnt. When all the vegetables and rice is mixed remove from stove.
4. Beat the eggs, pepper and salt till the mixture is white and foamy. Heat the balance 1/4 cup of oil and make several omelettes with the egg mixture in a small fry pan. Stack the omelettes and roll them together to form a jelly roll. Cut the omelette roll in to several strips and garnish the fried rice and serve with any curry dish of your choice.

KIRI BUTH-MILK RICE

Ingredients

- 2 cups of rice
- 1 can coconut milk(400 ml)
- 3 cups water
- 2 teaspoons salt

Directions

1. Wash rice well and place in a deep pan. Add water and cook the rice until the water boils and bubbles up. Mix the salt with the coconut milk and pour into the rice and mix well with a spoon(preferably a wooden spoon).
2. Cover the pan and cook on low heat until all the milk is absorbed. Pour the rice into a shallow dish and level with the spoon. Cut into square or diamond shape pieces.
3. If using a rice cooker: Wash rice, add water, rice, salt and coconut milk to the rice cooker and set the timer for cooking rice. Once cooked repeat the serving process.

- Jasmine rice or sticky white rice is recommended.

↖ Tamarind

SIYAMBALA BUTH-TAMARIND RICE

Ingredients

- 1 pound basmati rice (3 1/2 cups of rice)
- 3 onions
- 6 cardamoms
- 6 cloves
- 6 peppercorns
- ¼ cup ghee
- 1 sprig curry leaves
- ½ inch stem lemon grass
- 1/4 cup tamarind juice
- 1 inch cinnamon stick
- ½ teaspoon turmeric powder
- salt to taste

Directions

1. Wash the rice. Slice the onions and grind the cardamoms, cloves and peppercorns together. Heat the ghee and when hot, fry the onion, curry leaves and lemon grass, until onions are browned, then add the rice and stir fry for further 3 minutes.
2. Add ground peppercorn mix, tamarind juice, turmeric powder, and warm water as required and bring to boil. Cook over high heat for approximately 5 minutes, then reduce heat, cover pan and simmer until fragrant and rice is cooked. Serve with any curry of your choice.

BREADS

KOTTU-ROTI

Ingredients

- 1 pound godamba roti or parathas
- 1/4 cup grated carrots
- 1/4 cup finely chopped cabbage
- 1/4 cup finely chopped leeks
- 3 shallots
- 2 green chili
- 2 cloves of garlic
- 1 tsp of chopped ginger
- 1 tsp of cumin powder
- 1 tsp of chili powder
- 1/2 tsp of turmeric powder
- 3 pieces of curry chicken with gravy
- 1 cup oil
- 1 sprig curry leaves
- 1 inch piece of pandan leaf
- 1 inch stick of cinnamon
- salt to taste

Directions

1. Cut the godamba roti or parathas into strips. Separate gravy, debone and flake chicken. Finely chop shallots, green chili, ginger and garlic.
2. Heat oil and sauté the chopped shallots, chili, ginger, garlic, curry leaves, pandan leaf and cinnamon stick. Cook for about 5 minutes, add salt, cumin powder, chili powder, turmeric powder and continue to stir fry.
3. Reduce heat to medium and add chopped cabbage. Cook for 5 minutes mixing well, then add the chopped leak and continue to stir fry. Then add the carrots and cook till the vegetables are transparent and glossy.
4. Add the shredded chicken and repeat cooking till the chicken is a light golden brown.
5. Add the godamba roti or paratha strips. Keep mixing well while stir frying and lastly add the gravy. Cook for another 2-3 minutes till the gravy is absorbed well into the roti. Serve hot.

POL-ROTI COCONUT FLAT BREAD

Ingredients

- 1 pound all purpose flour
- 1 cup fresh grated coconut
- 1 stick unsalted butter or margarine
- 1/4 cup water
- salt to taste

Directions

1. Heat the butter/margarine with grated coconut in microwave for about 20 seconds. Mix the dissolved butter well with the coconut. Put flour into a deep mixing bowl and add the coconut mixture and mix well with flour to form crumbles.
2. Add water gradually to form a dough and add salt to taste. Knead well and form dough balls using your palms. Flatten the dough balls to form a round shape roti and cook on a hot griddle. Make sure to cook both sides evenly by constantly flipping the roti.
3. Serve with any curry or lunumiris(onion sambol).

- Add more water if the dough is dry but the dough shouldn't be sticky.
- Fresh grated coconut is available at Asian or Indian grocery stores.

PITTU

Ingredients

- 2 cups rice flour
- 1 cup freshly grated coconut
- 1/2 cup-water
- 1 cup of light coconut milk
- salt to taste

Directions

1. Mix the rice, freshly grated coconut, and salt in bowl. Add a spoon of water at a time and mix in circular motion to form little flakes or balls equal to the size of a grain of cooked rice. Once the mixture is flaked well cover the inside of a steamer with a piece of cheese cloth and steam it for about 10 minutes.
2. If you have a pittu mold, fill the mold with the mixture and steam for 10 minutes. Push the steamed pittu with a wooden spoon handle to a flat plate. Pour the coconut milk on the pittu and serve hot with curry.

- Amount of water needed depends on the quality and absorption rate of flour.
- Grated coconut is available in Asian grocery stores.
- Pittu mold-steamers are available for purchase online.
- Check equipment list for pittu mold-steamers.

APPA (HOPPERS)

Ingredients

- 2 1/2 cups of rice flour
- 1 1/2 cans of thick coconut milk (600 ml)
- 1/2 can of light coconut milk
- 2 teaspoons yeast
- 3 teaspoons of sugar
- 1/4 cup lukewarm water
- salt to taste
- 1/2 cup oil

Directions

1. Mix the yeast, and sugar with the lukewarm water and leave for about ten minutes to form bubbles. Then sieve the rice flour, salt into a bowl and mix with 1 can of thick coconut milk to make a batter. Add the yeast mixture, to the batter and mix well.
2. Cover the bowl and leave overnight. Take the batter out of the refrigerator about 3 hrs before making the hoppers. Cover the bowl and let the mixture rise. Mix the balance 1/2 can of thick coconut milk and 1/2 light coconut milk to the hopper batter and mix well just before you start. Coat the hopper pan with oil and heat it on medium heat. Pour a spoonful of batter into the heated pan and twist the pan in a circular motion.
3. Cover the pan till the middle portion is cooked and the edges turn light brown and crispy. Remove the appa with a metal spatula when done.
4. Egg appa can be cooked the same way with an egg in the middle. Remove from pan when the egg is cooked. Sprinkle with pepper and salt and serve hot.

- Check equipment list for appa (hopper) pans.

INDI APPA (STRING HOPPERS)

Ingredients

- 4 cups rice flour
- 2 1/4 cups of cold water
- 1 tsp of salt

Directions

1. Put the flour into brown paper bag and steam in a steamer for 1/2 hour flipping sides after 15 minutes. Take the flour out and put in a bowl and add the salt and mix well. Then add enough cold water gradually to form a dough that is not sticky.
2. Place a spoonful of dough. Into the string hopper mould and squeeze the dough onto a string hopper mat using a circular motion. Stack about 6 string hopper mats in a steamer and steam for 6-8 minuets.
3. Serve with curry and pol sambol.

- Pol sambol- coconut sambol.
- Check equipment list for string hopper mould/mats.

THOSAI

Ingredients

- 2 cups uludu dhal(black gram)
- 2 cups rice flour
- 1/2 cup parboiled rice
- 4 dried red chillies
- 2 shallots
- 1 tsp fenugreek
- 1 tsp cumin seeds
- 1 tsp salt
- 1/4 tsp turmeric powder
- 1/2 tsp baking soda
- 1 sprig curry leaves
- 1/4 cup oil

uludu dhal(black gram)

parboiled rice

Directions

1. Soak the uludhu dhal(black gram) and fenugreek in water until soft. Drain and grind the uludhu, fenugreek, parboiled rice and rice flour with enough water(add gradually) to make a batter similar to pancake batter.
2. Add salt, turmeric powder and baking soda to the batter and mix well again. Chop the onions, and break the dried chillies into pieces. On a separate pan heat 1/2 of the 1/4 cup oil, and fry the onion, dried chillies, curry leaves and cumin seeds for a few minutes making sure the dry chillies do not burn. Add to the batter and mix well.
3. Heat a griddle and coat it with oil and pour in batter to make a thosai. When holes appear on top, flip the thosai to cook the other side for a few minutes making sure it's not burned. Repeat the process till the batter is done.

EQUIPMENT LIST

Pittu Steamer

Wooden Spoons

Appa (Hopper) Pan

Griddle

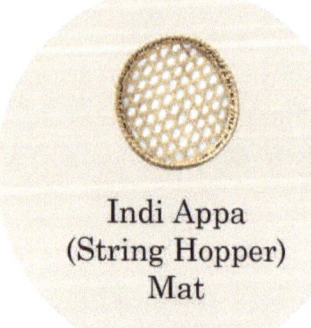
Indi Appa (String Hopper) Mat

Indi Appa (String Hopper) Mould

ACKNOWLEDGMENTS

Writing a book is harder than I thought and more rewarding than I could have ever imagined. None of this would have been possible without my awesome 86 yr old mother, Nalini Perera. She was the narrator for this series of Sri Lankan recipes during our mandatory quarantine for the COVID-19 pandemic of 2020.

Thank you to my brother Ananda Perera, who always cooked a feast for our families. His cooking gave me the chance to take photos to be included in my cookbooks.

A big thank you to my book designer Alexey Lavrentev of PhotoMagLab in Ukraine. His tireless efforts and creativity made it possible for me to publish this collection of authentic recipe books.

Above all, I'm eternally grateful for and thankful to my family: Manjula, Michael, Mikaile, Manjari, Mychal, Charith, Tracy, Ari, Suren, Diana and Freddie. You have always given me a reason to take the next step forward.

ABOUT THE AUTHOR

Shyamali Perera was born in Colombo, Sri Lanka, and emigrated to the United States in 1989 during Sri Lanka's civil war. She was an educator of young children for thirty years in Orange County, California. Her first book "Curry & Rice," was published as a Mother's Day gift in 2007, and was later published as an eBook in 2014. Presently she lives with her family in Southern California and continues to dedicate her time to, writing a variety of cookbooks and children's books.